SPOTLIGHT ON NATURE
GIRAFFE

MELISSA GISH

CREATIVE EDUCATION · CREATIVE PAPERBACKS

Published by Creative Education and Creative Paperbacks
P.O. Box 227, Mankato, Minnesota 56002
Creative Education and Creative Paperbacks are imprints
of The Creative Company
www.thecreativecompany.us

Design by Chelsey Luther; production by Joe Kahnke
Art direction by Rita Marshall
Printed in the United States of America

Photographs by Alamy (Anil Varma Photography, imageBROKER), Dream-
stime (Harperdrewart, Jocrebbin, Isaac Mcevoy, Szabolcs Stieber, Lorraine
Swanson), Getty Images (Shanna Baker/Moment, Manoj Shah/Photodisc,
Westend61), iStockphoto (Gleb_Ivanov, LeeYiuTung, Liudmyla Liudmyla),
Minden Pictures (Will Burrard-Lucas/NPL, Denis-Huot/NPL, Vincent
Grafhorst, Tony Heald/NPL, Juan Carlos Munoz/NPL, Winifried Wisniews-
ki), Oakland Zoo, Shutterstock (Hein Myers Photography, Noelle Herzog)

Library of Congress Cataloging-in-Publication Data
Names: Gish, Melissa, author.
Title: Giraffe / Melissa Gish.
Series: Spotlight on nature.
Includes index.
Summary: A detailed chronology of developmental milestones drives this life
study of giraffes, including their habitats, physical features, and conservation
measures taken to protect these towering land animals.
Identifiers: LCCN 2019056635 / ISBN 978-1-64026-338-3 (hardcover)
ISBN 978-1-62832-870-7 (pbk) / ISBN 978-1-64000-480-1 (eBook)
Subjects: LCSH: Giraffe—Juvenile literature. / Habitat conservation—
Juvenile literature.
Classification: LCC QL737.U56 G576 2020 / DDC 599.638—dc23

First Edition HC 9 8 7 6 5 4 3 2 1
First Edition PBK 9 8 7 6 5 4 3 2 1

CONTENTS

NUBIAN GIRAFFES

of Gambella National Park

In the far western corner of Ethiopia, on the border with South Sudan, lies the country's largest national park. Established in 1973, Gambella National Park covers nearly 1,800 square miles (4,662 sq km) of grasslands and forests. The Baro River, home to the rare shoebill stork, flows across its northern region. Unhindered by roads or fences, gentle giants—giraffes, elephants, and antelopes—roam the park.

It is early October, the start of *bega*, when seasonal rains cease and the floodplain and **savanna** begin to dry up. Members in a group of 24 Nubian giraffes—mostly female—use their lower front teeth like chisels to scrape thin sheets of bark from mango trees. One giraffe steps away from her companions, sensing the need for privacy. For 15 months, a baby giraffe has been growing inside her. The time has come for the calf to be born.

CLOSE-UP
Neck bones

Like humans, giraffes
have seven neck bones,
called cervical vertebrae.
These 10-inch-long (25.4
cm) bones are connected
by ball-and-socket joints
that allow the neck to be
highly flexible.

CHAPTER ONE

LIFE BEGINS

Giraffes are the tallest land mammals on Earth. Males, called bulls, typically stand 18 feet (5.5 m) tall and weigh about 2,800 pounds (1,270 kg). Females, called cows, are a few feet shorter and can weigh up to 2,000 pounds (907 kg). Newborn calves may be up to six feet (1.8 m) tall. They can stand within an hour of birth and run within 10 hours. It was once thought that only one kind of giraffe existed. In 2016, genetics helped researchers divide giraffes into four species—Masai, reticulated, southern, and northern—and into subspecies and ecotypes as well. Angolan and South African giraffes are subspecies of southern giraffes. Northern giraffe subspecies are Kordofan, West African, and Nubian. The giraffe's coat is covered with unique patches of dark fur

GAMBELLA NUBIAN GIRAFFE MILESTONES

DAY ①

- Born
- Able to stand and run
- Ossicones: flat, 1 inch (2.5 cm) long

- Height: 5.7 feet (1.7 m)
- Weight: 130 pounds (59 kg)

Welcome to the World

In Gambella National Park, the pregnant giraffe steps into a patch of sudan-grass that has grown more than eight feet (2.4 m) tall. Here she can be alone. Within about 30 minutes, her baby drops headfirst to the ground. Landing on his head after falling more than five feet (1.5 m) causes the calf to take his first breath. The baby giraffe bends his knees and rolls onto his belly. Sitting comfortably, he looks up at his mother as she reaches over to lick him clean.

separated by lines of lighter fur. The various types of giraffes can be distinguished by the colors and patterns of their coats. Giraffes have long legs and feet that are 12 inches (30.5 cm) across. Each foot has two toes covered by sharp hooves.

Adult giraffes face few threats but must protect young giraffes in their families from predators. Mother giraffes feed their youngsters milk, but then grown giraffes become herbivores. This means they eat only plants. They feed mainly on high-growing leaves, flowers, fruits, and tender twigs, which they grasp with their long, nimble tongues. A unique joint at the back of the skull allows giraffes to tip their heads straight back, extending their reach. Until they can access the highest treetops as adults, young giraffes

CLOSE-UP
Camouflaging coats

A giraffe's coat pattern helps it blend in with the tall grasses and shrubs of its environment. Like human fingerprints, patterns of markings are unique to each individual giraffe.

RHODESIAN GIRAFFE

SOUTHERN GIRAFFE

MASAI GIRAFFE

(3) WEEKS

- ▸ Introduced to herd
- ▸ First taste of vegetation
- ▸ Eyes: 2 inches (5.1 cm) in diameter
- ▸ Left with other calves while mother feeds

First Meal

Clean and dry, the Nubian giraffe calf stands up for the first time. He is only one hour old. Instinctively, he approaches his mother's belly. At nearly six feet (1.8 m) tall, the calf tilts his head upward and easily reaches the nipple that provides nourishing milk. The high fat content (about 12.5 percent) of giraffe milk will help the calf grow more than one inch (2.5 cm) every day for the first few weeks of his life. His mother will keep him hidden away during this time.

must compete with antelopes for the tenderest leaves closer to the ground.

Giraffes appear to have thick lips. This is because their lips, tongue, and mouth are coated in thick, hairlike projections that protect against the sharp thorns of their favorite trees, acacias. One of the giraffe's most unique features is the pair of bony structures on top of the head. These are called ossicones. Calves are born with soft, flexible ossicones made of tissue called cartilage. They are folded flat against the head to make the calf's birth easier. As giraffes age, the ossicones stand up and turn to bone, becoming part of the skull.

OSSICONE ············

CLOSE-UP
Ossicones

Unlike horns, ossicones are covered with skin and fur. And unlike antlers, ossicones are not shed seasonally. Bull giraffe ossicones are thicker and less hairy than those of cows. Bulls sometimes develop one to three additional ossicones with age.

(6) **MONTHS**

▸ Eating mostly vegetation
▸ Height: 7.5 feet (2.3 m)
▸ Weight: 195 pounds (88.5 kg)

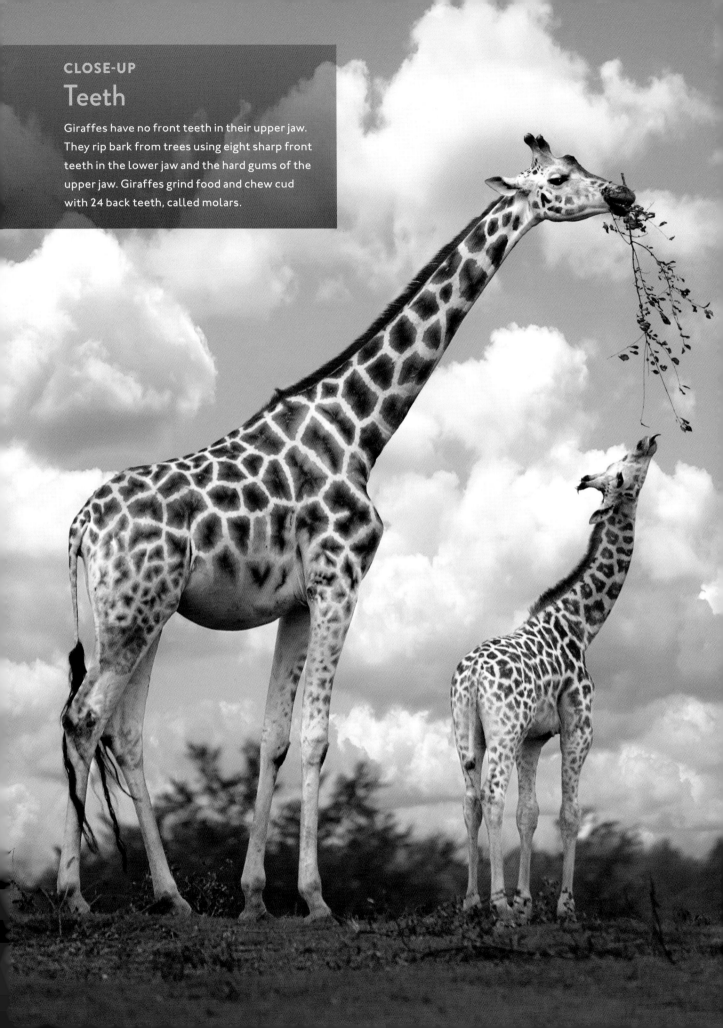

CLOSE-UP
Teeth

Giraffes have no front teeth in their upper jaw. They rip bark from trees using eight sharp front teeth in the lower jaw and the hard gums of the upper jaw. Giraffes grind food and chew cud with 24 back teeth, called molars.

CHAPTER TWO

EARLY ADVENTURES

Giraffes live in groups called herds. They are nomadic, meaning they do not stay in one place for very long. Although giraffes may feed on more than 100 different plants, their favorite food is acacia leaves. Mothers teach their youngsters the best leaves to eat. To protect themselves from being overbrowsed, acacia trees start to emit a bad taste if giraffes feed for too long. This keeps giraffes moving in search of tastier leaves. Despite having shorter legs, young giraffes have no trouble keeping up with their herd. Giraffes may feed for up to 18 hours a day—even in the dark. An adult giraffe may eat 100 pounds (45.4 kg) of vegetation daily.

Giraffes are the sentinels, or lookouts, of their animal communities. Their eyes are located on the sides of the head and protrude

(8) MONTHS

- No longer drinks milk
- Ossicones: 2.5 inches (6.4 cm) tall

Tongues

An adult giraffe's tongue is about 18 inches (45.7 cm) long. It can be dark purple to black. The tongue and lips work together like fingers to safely pluck food from thorny branches.

FEATURED FAMILY

Look Who's Tasting

It is mid-January in Gambella. Soon, the rainy season (*belg*) will begin. For now, though, the grass is dry, and leaves are sparse on the trees. The giraffe calf has joined six other youngsters in a group called a crèche. A few adults take turns babysitting, while others browse. Only three months old, the calf is not yet fully weaned. He cautiously licks some acacia leaves. Despite many weeks of trying, he has not yet mastered the skill of plucking them safely from between the tree's long thorns. A poke on his tongue startles him. He jerks his head back and rears up on his hind legs. He needs more practice.

Giraffes are the SENTINELS of their animal communities.

(1) YEAR

▸ Eyes: 4 inches (10.2 cm) in diameter
▸ Height: 11 feet (3.4 m)
▸ Weight: 280 pounds (127 kg)

slightly. Giraffes can see much of the world around them without having to turn their heads. Their height also gives them an obvious advantage. Knowing this, their neighbors—buffaloes, zebras, antelopes, and even baboons—rely on giraffes to provide early warning of approaching predators. Despite living in a herd, giraffes typically do not form close bonds. There is no leader who tells the rest of the herd when to move on. Each giraffe simply remains within eyesight of the others in its herd. Mothers and their calves are the exceptions. They stick close together.

FEATURED FAMILY

Give It a Try

In June, at the height of the rainy season, or *kiremt*, the floodplain is filled with water. The grasslands and forests are lush and green. The calf spends much of his day eating leaves and flower buds. His mother has shown him which ones to select, and he has gained control of his tongue. Reaching out, the tip of his tongue curls around a feathery pink blossom and plucks it from a mimosa tree. This is a sweet seasonal treat.

$\textcircled{4}$ **YEARS**

- ▸ Becomes an older brother
- ▸ Eats 55 pounds (24.9 kg) of vegetation daily

CLOSE-UP
Sleeping

Giraffes sleep no more than two hours each day. Sleep consists of naps that last no longer than five minutes at a time. Most giraffes sleep standing up. Some lie down, their neck curled to rest on their back. Giraffes take turns standing guard.

CHAPTER THREE

LIFE LESSONS

Most giraffe herds have 10 to 20 members, but some have as many as 50 where food is abundant. When they have places to go, giraffes can walk 10 miles (16.1 km) per hour. They can run 35 miles (56.3 km) per hour, though they rarely do so. Instead, herds usually amble from tree to tree, traveling about 10 miles (16.1 km) each day as they browse. Older bulls, isolating themselves from herds, may travel a little farther. As long as there are no cows in the area, bulls get along with each other and may even form smaller, males-only herds.

Giraffes do not have a specific mating season. Usually, they choose to mate when food is plentiful. Cows can mate by age five, but bulls are typically six or seven before they mate. Older bulls may beat up and chase away younger bulls in order to keep cows to themselves.

(6) YEARS	(7) YEARS
▸ Joins herd of young males	▸ Wins necking battle
▸ Engages in necking	▸ Mates for the first time
▸ Fails to win the battle	▸ Ossicones: 7 inches (17.8 cm) tall

Fathers do not participate in the care of their offspring and typically ignore youngsters. Mothers band together in nursery groups to help each other protect their calves from predators. Most calves are weaned between 7 and 10 months. They become more independent as their browsing skills develop. Females typically remain in their family herd, but by the time bulls are mature, they have left.

Giraffes have few natural predators. Lions and leopards may target young giraffes but usually avoid adults. Each of the giraffe's feet is 12 inches (30.5 cm) across. One kick can kill a lion. Giraffes also have huge hearts. The organs are nearly 2 feet (0.6 m) long and weigh about 24

FEATURED FAMILY

This Is How It's Done

At the height of another dry season in Gambella, the young giraffe is now two years old. He watches with curiosity as a new calf is introduced to the herd. Suddenly, the tall, brittle grass rustles. A leopard steps forward, its eyes on the calf. Several adults turn their backs on the leopard and begin to kick their hind legs. The leopard slinks away. From a safe distance, the young giraffe mimics his companions' action. The day will soon come when he will need to defend himself in this way.

Each of a giraffe's feet is **12 INCHES** ←-----across.-----→ One **kick** can kill a **LION.**

 YEARS

- Begins wandering from herd
- Powerful kicks used as defense
- Height: 17 feet (5.2 m)
- Weight: 2,200 pounds (998 kg)

12 YEARS

- Lives mostly alone
- Father to numerous offspring
- Height: 17.5 feet (5.3 m)
- Weight: 2,500 pounds (1,134 kg)

pounds (10.9 kg). Giraffes have the strongest known blood pressure of any animal. A giraffe's heart beats about 170 times per minute, pumping 20 gallons (75.7 L) of blood through its body. Extra-tight skin squeezes giraffe legs like stockings, which prevents blood from settling in their long limbs.

CLOSE-UP
Necking

Swinging their necks, bulls smack each other with their heads. This behavior, called necking, is a fight for mating rights. Usually one bull gives up and walks away, but fierce fights can lead to injury and even death.

FEATURED ——— FAMILY

Practice Makes Perfect

Taking a break from browsing, the young giraffe has joined other young males in a game of play-necking. They rear up on their back legs and lift their front legs to tap each other on the shoulder. Their swinging necks bend and twist. They bop each other with their heads. Such play helps strengthen muscles and improve coordination. In a few more years, as mature bulls, they will try to knock down opponents. For now, though, the young males are just having fun.

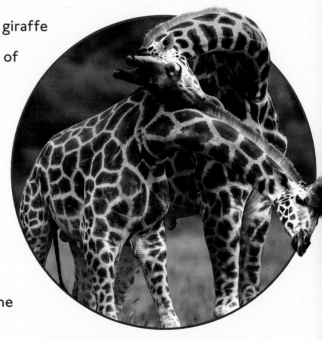

(15) YEARS	(19) YEARS	(25) YEARS
▸ Weakened during drought ▸ Survives lion attack ▸ Height: 18 feet (5.5 m) ▸ Weight: 2,700 pounds (1,225 kg)	▸ Eats 90 pounds (40.8 kg) of vegetation daily ▸ Ossicones: 10 inches (25.4 cm) tall	▸ End of life

CHAPTER FOUR

GIRAFFE SPOTTING

Giraffes once numbered in the millions and roamed throughout much of Africa, but their numbers have drastically declined recently. Some subspecies are near extinction. As humans spread deeper into wilderness areas, habitat loss and fragmentation threaten giraffe populations. Buildings and fences are constructed, and forests are razed for farming, logging, and mining. As food disappears and giraffe populations become cut off from each other, the animals are less able to locate mates or are forced to mate with nearby giraffes. This inbreeding causes genetic weaknesses that can lead to the extinction of giraffes in that area.

One strategy for rebuilding healthy giraffe populations involves moving giraffes to protected habitats in order to broaden the genetic makeup of those areas. Once stretching across Africa from Senegal to Eritrea, West African giraffes dropped to only 49 individuals by the 1990s. The government of Niger and several conservation groups worked together to move giraffes to such places as the Gadabedji

Biosphere Reserve. Thanks to these efforts, there are now about 600 West African giraffes.

In 2016, researchers with the Giraffe Conservation Foundation were concerned that most of Uganda's Rothschild's giraffes lived north of the Victoria Nile River in Murchison Falls National Park. In hopes of establishing another population center, 37 giraffes were captured and ferried across the river. Within only a few years, several new calves were born, signaling the success of the translocation. Similar efforts are needed throughout Africa. From 1985 to 2015, the overall giraffe population plummeted by 40 percent. Since 2000, giraffes have completely disappeared from at least seven African nations and have drastically declined in seven others.

Despite some conservation victories, giraffes suffer greatly from poaching. In nations where giraffes exist, many people struggle with civil war and poverty, and a giraffe can provide a great deal of food. Although rangers patrol protected areas and dismantle traps and snares, poachers are often a step ahead of such efforts. Conservationists worry that the public is unaware of how desperate the giraffe's situation has become. Large-scale conservation efforts are needed throughout Africa if giraffes are to once again safely and sustainably roam their traditional homelands.

SNAPSHOTS

About 15,780 **reticulated giraffes** live in southern Somalia, southern Ethiopia, and northern Kenya. They have brownish-orange patches separated by thick white lines.

Creamy brown with dark brown, leaf-shaped patches on their coats, **Masai giraffes** are the darkest species. Most of the remaining 35,000 reside in Kenya and Tanzania.

The critically endangered **Nubian giraffe** has large, reddish-brown rectangular patches. About 650 of the surviving 3,000 live in Ethiopia and South Sudan.

The roughly 1,100 **Rothschild's giraffes**, found in Kenya and Uganda, are an ecotype of **Nubian giraffe**.

The **Rhodesian giraffe**, a **Masai giraffe** ecotype, is found nowhere else but Zambia's South Luangwa Valley, where its population totals about 550.

In 2017, 1.2 million YouTube viewers watched a live stream of April, a **reticulated giraffe**, giving birth at Animal Adventure Park.

Kordofan giraffes have pale, irregular patches and white legs. About 2,000 are scattered throughout five war-torn central African nations.

The **South African giraffe** has star-shaped patches. About 37,000 inhabit Angola, Botswana, Mozambique, Namibia, South Africa, Zambia, and Zimbabwe.

An estimated 17,750 **Angolan giraffes** are found in Botswana, Namibia, and western Zimbabwe. They are light-colored with large, jagged patches.

BENGHAZI

Benghazi was a **reticulated giraffe** who painted pictures by holding a brush in his mouth. Born at the Oakland Zoo in California, he lived there for 23 years.

Scientists studied **Rothschild's giraffes** in three European zoos and recorded the rare low-frequency hums and groans of giraffe vocalizations.

George, a 19-foot-tall (5.8 m) **Masai giraffe** who lived at Chester Zoo in England from 1959 to 1969, was the tallest giraffe on record.

Found only in Niger, **West African giraffes** have rectangular light-tan patches separated by thick, cream-colored lines. Their pale lower legs have no markings.

Zarafa, a **Nubian giraffe** given to King Charles X of France by the ruler of Egypt in 1827, lived for 20 years. Her body is on display at a natural history museum in La Rochelle, France.

WORDS to Know

ecotypes — distinct forms of a plant or animal species that has changed to improve its chances of survival in a particular environment

endangered — at risk of dying out completely

extinction — the state of having died off completely

genetics — of or relating to genes (the basic units of heredity)

inbreeding — the breeding of individuals that are related to one another

mammals — animals that have a backbone and hair or fur, give birth to live young, and produce milk to feed their young

poaching — hunting protected species of wild animals, even though doing so is against the law

savanna — a grassy, mostly treeless plain in tropical or subtropical regions

species — a group of living beings with shared characteristics and the ability to reproduce with one another

weaned — accustomed to food other than milk

LEARN MORE

Books

Bozzo, Linda. *How Giraffes Grow Up*. New York: Enslow, 2020.

Raatma, Lucia. *Giraffes*. New York: Children's Press, 2014.

Smith, Lucy Sackett. *Giraffes: Towering Tall*. New York: PowerKids Press, 2010.

Websites

"Facts About Giraffe." Giraffe Conservation Foundation. https://giraffeconservation.org/facts/.

"Giraffe." National Geographic. https://www.nationalgeographic.com/animals/mammals/g/giraffe/.

"Giraffe." San Diego Zoo Animals & Plants. https://animals.sandiegozoo.org/animals/giraffe.

Documentaries

Mustill, Tom. "Giraffes: Africa's Gentle Giants." *Nature*, season 35, episode 3. Thirteen Productions, BBC, WNET, 2016.

Reid, Alison. *The Woman Who Loves Giraffes*. Free Spirit Films, 2018.

Scott Davison, Ashley. *Catching Giants*. Iniosante Studios, 2018.

Visit

AFRICAN LION SAFARI

Home to more than 1,000 animals, including Canada's largest giraffe herd.

1386 Cooper Road
Cambridge, ON
Canada N1R 5S2

CHEYENNE MOUNTAIN ZOO

See the largest reticulated giraffe herd in the U.S., and hand-feed the gentle giants.

4250 Cheyenne Mountain Zoo Road
Colorado Springs, CO 80906

LOUISVILLE ZOO

Visitors can stand face-to-face with the tallest mammals on Earth and feed them.

1100 Trevilian Way
Louisville, KY 40213

WILDLIFE SAFARI

A variety of African animals roam this 600-acre (243 ha), drive-through park.

1790 Safari Road
Winston, OR 97496

INDEX